I0692173

# A Plea to a Wine Cork

## and other

## happenstances

## By Jim Ross

Scriptline Images
Beret Imprint
21740 El Puma Cir
Sonora, CA 95370

Copyright © 2016 by Jim Ross. All rights reserved.
Printed in the United States of America. No part of this
book may be used or reproduced in any manner
whatsoever without written permission except in the case
of brief quotations embodied in critical articles and
reviews. For information address Scriptline Images,
21740 El Puma Circle, Sonora, CA 95370.

Library of Congress Cataloging-in-Publication Data Ross,
Jim (James Lee), 1941--
Scattered Reflections: poetry

Includes bibliographical references and index.
ISBN: 978-0-9978003-2-6
1. poetry. 2. Rhyme. xxx.x'x—dcxx

ASIN: B01JTIJXA6

## Dedication

For Ginny, who paints a breathtaking curl!

## Epigraph

*Not knowing the future, and savoring its
presences event by event,
is only seconded by the mind's steeped
reflections of their images*

—Jim Ross

# Contents

# Part I

## The Birth of a Seafarer

Here heels the sailboat-on-wheels over floors
pushed by a young hand
shouting pleas, good Lord, for *sailors to move*
and be lively, too, before the wind shifts over
the briny brew.
Now he has my mind wrapped in a pea coat,
for the ride of rides—on his fine sailboat, the
mast takes on length, the carpet turns blue so
the sea can heave as we roll on through.
I swear I smell salt by the time we hear ...
*Dinner is ready*. *Wash up and come here.* We
did. It is good, but sailing is best. *Tuck me in,
Grandpa, it's time for my rest.*

## Tomorrow Gently Grows

Fourteen fine acorns interrupted from their
chore by a child's small hands,
held cupped for gentle display--acorns safe in
angel wings

## First Light

Peachy smears of sky
set nature's stage above
brittle autumn crisps
of naked, nervous shapes—
silvered cameos framed
by liquid sheets of transformed beach
for virgin eyes first glance at ice
and frost and what awaits the day

## A Cherub and I

A cherub and I
meet on a day in the park
and he studies me

## The Book Not Read

The pages riffled
by a baffled preschooler
net a joyous laugh
at the whir of blurred paper—
entertainment beyond words

## Sissy Takes a Trip

Mom's green hat with feather snippets
bob in a flowered chapeau band;
on Sissy's head, a grand exhibit,
Mom's green hat with feather snippets,
yellow shoes with nylon anklets,
Sissy moves to far off wonderlands—
Mom's green hat with feather snippets
bob in a flowered chapeau band.

## Inquisitive

Mind and eyes agape
at never before seen sights
of fantastic shapes
called trees, which shiver when blown
and birds that flutter and rise

## Butterfly Ballet

Draw me not from the cocoon of my change
and make of me an omelet. Rather, let my
colors unfold glossy and wet, and when
I dry have me fly through the ether, whole,
to flit as nature wills.
Watch me at a distance as one in the light of
the universe.

## Independent Fellow

*Hello*
*my friend, you cat*
*whose coat is slick and smooth,*
*you come and go at will so now*
*goodbye*

## Curtain Hangers

Feisty
kitty frolics
blurred in a carpet chase
gone vertical on fine drapery
who then hang as wavering balls of fur
competitive sibling exploits
driven at warp speed down
by squirt bottle—
feisty

## Attitude Forever

As slow footfalls crunch,
the dog stares wide-eyed, silent,
high-centered in snow.

He treads to the bush,
blackberry eyes watch him come.
Entwined he waits.

Gee-Chu the Lhasa
towers over many things,
anthills, fallen leaves.

## The Power of Muse

She spews forth the word
and the paper is painted
with lines of meaning
that reaches wizards of words
for their arsenal of light

## Mountain Hospitality

Aspen
wait as befits
a rooted shade-giver,
patiently shivering: *Welcome*
*overheated hikers with salty lips*
*who echo craggy mountain-tales,*
*who hear the breezy hush*
*and breathe scented*
*aspen*

## Museum Demonstration

Shivers and shocks,
devastation of blocks of homes,
large and small, businesses by the score,
roadbeds re-sculptured in three axis shifts
for the pleasure of rides, *whoopee-do* and otherwise.
What I get, is fits of *mal de mer*
with purges befitting the wavering occasion
of earth's course slippage
as she prunes in her crusty dotage
taking on a new face for all to see.

## Superlatives

One has to take pity
on the poor superlative;
it is just doing its job when
it extols the virtue of the best activities
and sights.
Still, I admit to headaches,
like reading after eating too much sugar—
(the apple pie and steaming coffee were
delicious) then the magnificent superlative
makes my teeth grate until I fall into a
troubled sleep. Perhaps it's the whole
adjective thing—
find a powerhouse noun or verb, if you will,
and forget the rest—*Mercy*!

## The First Snowman

Dwindling snow defiled by youthful
exuberance digging and tamping
a snowman of any size—
quick, before the last snow melts

## Hothouse Allegiance

Brilliant green lilies
greet the climbing winter sun
with unfurled acclaim

## Twice Arrested by a Verb

Now I find a verb and am arrested
by its awesome power--how it can run
on paper, fleet, as thoroughbreds attest on
thundering hooves till the race is won;  horses
merely subjects for the fun--
objects casting shadows, making meanings,
blow their wind across sweating, slickened
duns, pricked to run through life governed by
feelings

## The Chastening

Now I am stripped of words' splendid bequest,
and live the toil of workdays won,
marked by paychecks stacked as prime
endpoint gestes, now building models to soar
beyond bastions
in lengthy blue flights, strangely barren
to eyes that know loftier, penned blessings
I'd forsaken—these daily flights a mere crawl to
chasten;
pricked to run through life governed by
feelings.

## Taffy's Cinematic Dream

Taffy dreams of catching bugs
up there on the big silver screen,
leaping long to snatch black flies
before the unforgiving lens—
lithe and strong, paws flashing in air..
Taffy knows he can do it, time after time.
He dreams he'll *make it big*, he'll make Morris
past history,  a mere footnote...
when Taffy shines.

## Dignified Sage

And now
I rise a man
of stature, tall and broad,
with baritone voice to be heard,
bathing


## Playing Outside

Stirred awake to learn rhythmic cycles,
warm and cool by vibrating turns—
as if coming from within and spilling
over my nose
a presence bestows movement
with pleasant pressures on my ears and eyes—
breaking softly on my face
in warm, sweet, meaningful waves
over and over I hear the sound—*wind* spoken—when
the pressure comes—so I think *wind* as it breaks and
rolls small bugs on the ground


## Life on Nut Lane

The jay swooped down, loudly squawking,
the squirrel raced off, hardly balking,
to the nest was the goal,
the nut dropped in the hole,
the exploit well-marked by proud barking.

## Within, Without

Safe within the castle, tall--
blocky, rocky home and self-made jail
to keep marauders out,
gives rise to wistful cries for strolls outside the
walls where all is touched by gentle skies of
shifting, broken puffs of heaven's hue

Suffused winds blow and whistle of a night,
down corridors, strong, and twisting, long, to
reach the hearts within the safety of the keep,
to touch their souls with nameless aches and
sleepless times...
to ponder what they miss—or not

## From the Pier

Seagulls
squawk overhead
when bait is skewered and cast—
*whirring* meat to the white-capped sea,
for fish

## Message from Home

Here in my sweeping conifer bowl
rolling with a will for home,
I spy wind-brushed wisps of gold-tinged clouds
playing with a lined, translucent moon
full against a pool of deep cyan.
This is the ecosystem of my life
and I am swelled in awe, inspired again
to love it fully, think deeply and care for
it as I can.

# Part II

## Fool Me Twice...Brr!

Cold by remembrance
the lightly lapping ocean
taunts a tempted soul
to make the uncertain plunge
and reunite with the truth

## Summer's Scent

Rapture captures my heart, my mind,
by breezes sent with fragrance sweet,
mixed sure to lure romance and bind
rapture captures my heart, my mind.

Truth fair, sweet air, eyes closed to blind
what matters not; this lover's treat...
rapture captures my heart, my mind,
by breezes sent with fragrance, sweet

## Waste Not My Love

'Neath a star spray
pulled by a rising silver moon
neath a star spray
I beg your forgiveness to stay lover,
lest your loss beg a swoon
from me, your prodigal buffoon
neath a star spray

## Humble Droplets

Now beads the spring-stream
as does man's perspiration
in light of the sun

## As One

Tender, guides her suitor in his tug
to a wondrous place of unobstructed view;
where misty vistas clear and
all things seen are gloriously new.

Hopeful, he points beloved to a place upon a
spit of greening land that sips at the loche.
She nods, he grins; now both can know the
grandeur of new love that has a place . . .

Sanguine clasps of hands held tight, with
eyes in common-vision locked, and hearts
that beat one rhythm, true, for life to fill as
coupled joy, unlocked . . .

as far as eyes can see,
as far as minds can reach,
as far as any love can feel
on a journey of this kind...
as one

## Situation

Balmy summer day
fragrant breeze to stir one's soul
to share pleasantries

## Quan Yin's Garden

Protected by stones
she contemplates life's vastness
by a tiny pond

## Getting Through It

Brutish lad with canted crown
seeks to woo with hands on hips
while in return milady frowns
and purses sour lips.

Crushed, the gaudy, jilted swain
bends his will to understand
what he did to be a bane
left with a hollow golden band.

Forlorn and huddled on a bench
his crown doffed upon the slats
milady sees with painful wrench
his plight is hers--her love-eyes bat.

So now in dappled shade he kneels,
While milady blushes, saying how she feels.

## Earring Play

When rays of sun or beams of moon
strike clothes,
make yellow, gold, and purple mauve
delights,
when wind eddies and gently flips
light hems,
long hair behind fair trumpets curve,
bangles
frolic in sight for all to know
the joy
of nature's high, and dancing wild
with you.

## Heavenly Spears

Moon quills scribe their joy
 on candlelit patios
 for dancing lovers


## Fly By

From first
 to last your words
 send thrills as they flutter
 from the page to do your bidding
 for love

## Collaboration

Boulders grind to sand
relentless monotony
sunset flames the sea
torches bathers poised for art
sans toes mingled with new friends

## Summer Passes

Scorching wind takes toll
whips brittle grass beyond gold
dies for August night

## Will-o-the-Wisp

Ignis fatui
sneezes phosphorescent light and pungent
ethers
of nature's alchemic mood into a misty
swamp night

## Homage to the Great Franklin

Did you see the young lad named Benny
scoop from the street, errant pennies?
He then placed them in jars and ran
laughing, afar,
to banks where they now grow aplenty!

## A Plea to a Wine Cork

I understand wine cork your years of toil,
your years of devotion,
your purpose to let the wine not spoil;
the nectar in the bottle you protect
with yourself is an unselfish thing, indeed!

But aged wine cork, please . . .
when the time comes and your end is near,
remain unselfish one more moment, too!

let the corkscrew skewer your body
and lift you gently out,
let your dignity prevail,
let your body come wholly out.

Do you know what awaits you
if you don't pass the test?

A tea strainer, for tea leaves!

I'll do my part, wine cork,
yes, however small,
To drink the wine and love the girl,
and dance to music, bright;
if you'll do yours, above and beyond,
and not let cork parts float.

This is my thank you, wine cork; ahead of
time, this is my plea: let me keep the lady
enthralled, and the wavering candles tall,
and your memory forever enshrined to me.

## Song of Striving

In the foothills high where miners trod
a clump of grass waves over sod,
salutes the dirt once pitched by man—
that somehow plays with heaven's plan.

They came and went with earthly gold,
they told their tales within their folds,
so others came, found none to pan--
that somehow plays with heaven's plan.

It all is clear to those who hear
the whistles driven to the ear;
to sights we're left to see and scan—
that somehow plays with heaven's plan.

*I've got to know*, the footloose say,
then trip out lightly on their way
to find out how to make a fan--
that somehow plays with heaven's plan.

The good news here--the grass still grows!
Man still strives, heaven knows.

A puzzle to work an answer that's grand.
That somehow plays with heaven's plan.

The day is done and darkness falls
there's chatter now within the halls,
good cheer reigns dear within the clan;
that somehow plays with heaven's plan!

Adventure's flame flashes for all--
some even heed the siren's call
and rush to sail catamarans
that somehow plays with heaven's plan.

The flame of life so boldly told
between the bible's leather folds
is bowed to by the common man--
That somehow plays with heaven's plan!

There's plenty more for this long list,
the message pitch rings in the mist
to fill the time within our spans
That somehow plays with heaven's plan.

## Love's Journey

Cow eyes, preacher's words,
sun and moon in union blessed,
replete, joyous years

## First Word

Fingers twirl the pen
pinched above the dazzling page—
unblemished, daring

## Still Searching for You

Beyond the fire's light,
beyond the swirling night
you are there for me

## Best Boy

Today we're on location
in the boonies, lugging gear.
Sometimes it's hell, this vocation—
missteps lead sweat and fear!

In the boonies, lugging gear
far from parts to help my station,
missteps lead sweat and fear--
*faux pas* leave no abrasion?

Far from parts to help my station,
the glaring star will shave careers!
*faux pas* leave no abrasion? *When
the lizard wears cashmere!*

The glaring star will shave careers;
I fix her glasses while she raves;
when the lizard wears cashmere
will she bend to me, behave.

I fix her glasses while she raves;
she thrusts them on and leers.
Will she bend to me, behave?
*You lovely man, I'm just veneer!*

I persevere as nervous gadgeteer;
sometimes it's hell, this vocation—
I triple check my gear--
today we're on location!

## Star Gazer

Oak leaves resting in a field,
benign composting stuff
beneath the trees that grew them—
lurks the rake of doom,
his passport to the stars

## Vulnerable

The knife's edge whetted for work unfit
to keep the vulnerable ridge
aligns with strivers battling windmills
with swords—always blunted and chipped

## Icy Snippets

Collars up, brown goatees dusted snowy
gray,
chores done in wind-flapped coats
along canyons of steel and glass that
resonates with traffic-horns, shouts and
Christmas music blare

Mother laughing, small boy jumping
m a k i n g it hard for her to hold his mittened
hand as he moves with unabashed glee
from toys behind the glistening window wall
to mother's bright-eyed face

Lengthening strides speed the pace through
stores replete with everything
but what the kestrel-eyed shoppers want—
preying more than thinking, now
to snag the only perfect Christmas gift

A pink-cheeked lady in a bustling
coffeehouse quickly sets her steaming
coffee down,
sits and lets a long contented sigh;
her eyes grow soft as she parts a festive
bag, oblivious to other's nearby, kindred
sighs

## A Step Away

A step away from life's long work,
deep shadows loom where unknowns lurk;
a decision is made, a quick trip west
to mask the fear, move fast, with zest;
no time to play--shun slothful quirks!
I'm just a step away.

Find the tempo, don't go berserk,
with new careers, release is work;
I sigh and know the truth is rest,
but this at best is just
a step away.

An angel comes as coffee perks
and makes me smile, I'm hardly irked.
I'm not going. *No, I'm not pressed*!
Then breathe-in flight, you know the rest:
crusades await my handiwork—
just a step away.

## Tides of Love and Loss

We swore our oaths with smiles, when ocean
surf ran high,
when crested, running seas crashed lullabies
nearby.
Beholders saw our vows, they strained so
hard to hear above the salty sea breeze,
the words we didn't hear.

Tides, tides of love and loss
swell our hearts and breaks them, tides fix
our ills and make us cry, the highs and lows
between them.

Ebb reveals a rocky shore
where stifling tide pools flush
as fleeting fools of passion, lust, in sun-
wrought super-blush,
we stab the life of love we had 'neath covers
softly spread
for someone else's skin— we lie our truths
abed.

Tides, tides of love and loss,
swell our hearts and breaks them. Tides fix
our ills and make us cry, the highs and lows
between them.

Love can't live with tawdry lies nor lover's
broken hearts, nor footprints in wet sand
in rushing ocean starts.
We hug, then sadly part, the
teardrops flow and melt,
within the surf's last froth
love's last moments dwell.

Tides, tides of love and loss,
swell our hearts and breaks them. Tides fix
our ills and make us cry, the highs and lows
between them.

### Reflection Pond

The lake at the top of my world
is not the highest collection
of water in the world--Titicaca, in the
Peruvian Andes
holds that lofty, distinction—but those
waters, rippled by wispy South American
air reveal secrets to my soul the way my
lower placed, lake of meltwater has.

To admit, by comparison, my lake is not the
lowest of fresh water congeries, either;
the Sea of Galilee, in Israel claims that title
and besides, my proud little lake would not
wish to relocate to the sub-sea level and
have to maintain such an historic profile
as the place of the ministry of Christ.

It is enough that people arrive to sit on
the little lake's banks and drink deeply,
the water and sky, then move on refreshed
—sometimes wondering why.

It could be the clearest small lake for a
very short time every year, when a roaring
spring runoff of alpine cascades transfuses
new life into in her polished, crystal eye:

the eye that collects and reflects the peaks
above it, endlessly transforming the lake

into a watery chameleon--now with a
flock of geese passing, now with a
lightning-bolt in a Zeusian-ripped sky. It
reveals a vision of its own banks reflected
and real.

No, the lake is only one of many, and its
clarity is reserved for souls who gaze upon it
and find love.

Two dueling lake-giants stake their
perennial claim in this matter of
transparency:
Lake Kussharo speaks to its purity in
accents of Hokkaido, loud and clear, and
competes
across the white capped waves of the
Pacific,
with the wizard of Crater Lake letting it
know it opposes Oregon's claim;

The wizard translates Japanese with the
fluency of his ilk then dips his feet
beneath equally clear skies, all in his calm
certainty that the water of his perfect crater
cannot be bested;

There are many other things the lake at the
top of my world is not, and the "nots" are
significant if you want to float an ocean
liner through it to traverse a continent and
sell a cargo of whatnots where you will;

It is not suited to host an Olympic
swimming event, as a dive from its banks—
even the flat dive of a Speedo clad
swimmer will leave the diver unhappy with

the granite scrapings of endeavor;

It is also not silent most times of the day—
hummingbirds and dragonflies see to that
as they flit through native brush with other,
more nefarious pilots, like mosquitoes and
flies—

The exception comes when the arc of the
sun is a mere pinpoint of light in the rocky
saw-tooth west; at its daily death and
rebirth it leaves ears to ring in premier
silence, that time when the silent pitch
entices a glance to gape at the even larger
granite bowl, scarred by ice and earth-shift,
inside which, the little jewel sits, to scan
that vast stretch of majestic earth—just
stone, carved earth's way, Man's gaudy
ornaments nowhere in sight.

Then the first raptors swoop through the
spirals of their lives, spreading ripples as
they greet trout. The stillness is gone and I
remember—

The lake at the top of my world is just a
lake
with only those who know it, happy it
exists,
and happier still to share its worth with
friends.

## Take My Poem, Not My Chips!

It's a kind of scary bug, a tiny, mysterious
thing that sweeps along on multiple feet— a
vision in orange and white bands
in synchronous glide--

like a lady en-gowned from head to toe,
who glides in her getup across hardwood, down
halls, her moves flat, without bob—.
perhaps a slight weave as direction demands

the lady's purpose is clear--it usually is--
where the bug-moves seem fruitless
as it endlessly glides down and up, side to side,
across and into—*what*?

Which leaves one to wonder if it goes till it
drops--no eating, unreasonable, no stopping
for this thing or that?

I don't have the interest, the right kind of time,
to follow the blighter to the end of its time, yet
still, it is graceful, arresting to watch as it
climbs to the cupboard and goes for a peek,
inside amongst jars,
sealed cans it can't breach.

But other things there, bagged with loose
folded tops--the chips, the cookies,
the sprinkles, whatnot, give one reason for
pause, eyebrows to rise—

Should its small life be ended right here, and
right now?
No! And here's why—but don't call me *bug-
wuss* when I tell you the truth;

I'd been gripping a sheet of something far
worse—a page of bad rhyme—
foolscap of no worth—evidence, my friends,
of poetic dearth!

So I flatten the page before tireless bug feet,
then beg its forgiveness as it climbs on
aboard-- for the short, fibrous ride on black,
spoiled ink, outside.

Now in fresh air, with bug company to keep, it
moves from the page without pause, without
sleep, over orange and white friends, tangled
legs without end, into compost as thick as it
needs.

I then crumple the page and push it beneath
brown molding leaves, over bugs going
nowhere, but me going home!
Home to my bug-free grub!

## Lake Lustrous Tale

With the flip of a tail,
the biggest trout I've ever seen
takes my breath away and
makes my hopeful heart race
with the pace of a thoroughbred.
Faster, I definitely think,
than any human heart should go!
It takes the line and drags it around the lake in
strained  zigzags of coded import,
spelled in spreading wakes that finally slow.
I reel him in, pride swelling my heart;
*Pisces Gargantua,* I call the trout, and soon
the truth is revealed, and my eyes pop.
He eyes me back as I reach to haul him in

But he flips the hook away as if he'd just been
holding it for this moment.

His tail slaps the water and he disappears,
leaving me breathless and with a toothpick
of a hook to tell my tale—
which no one believes, of course.
Thankful he left me with rod and reel,
line intact, to dream of a lucky day ahead, I'll
be armed with a shiny new hook.

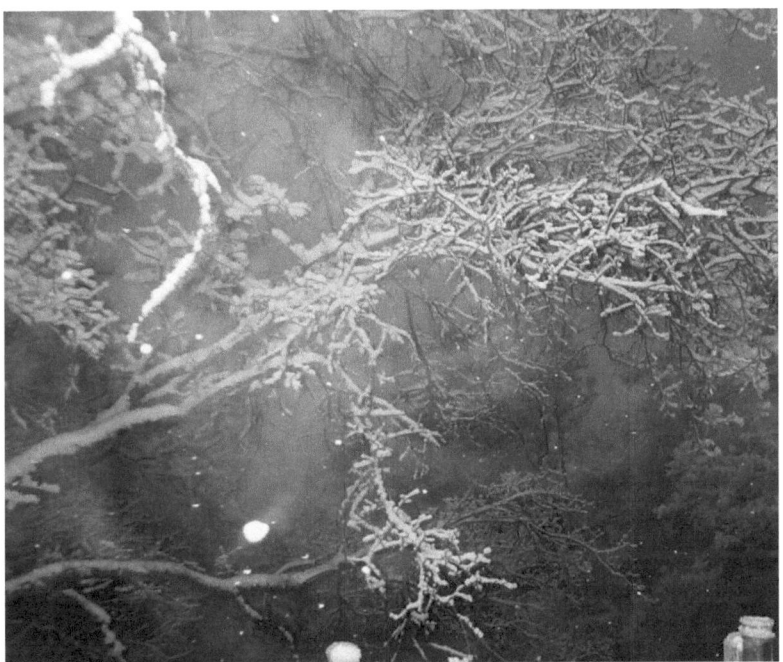

## Winter Camp

Here in the evening
with cold—a surrounding snow—
and warmth, flaming wood
crackling by my stockinged feet,
snuggly in my rural keep

## Within, Without

Safe within the castle, tall—
blocky, rocky home and self-made jail
to keep marauders out,
gives rise to wistful cries
for strolls outside the walls
where all is touched
by gentle skies of shifting,
broken puffs of deepest hue

Suffused winds blow and
whistle of a night, down corridors, strong, and
twisting, long,
to reach the souls within
the safety of the keep,
to touch their souls
with nameless aches
and sleepless times to ponder
what they miss—or not...

## North Wind Foe

Caps of waves foam-white,
run south with the icy wind
to break on slick decks
and sailors who ply great ships
north to their havens, their berths

## Surfeit Most Sublime

My heart is full,
my head is stuffed;
I am glutted by all things good.
You dazzle my eyes, squeeze my hands, scent
my dreams, honey my tongue, lilt in my ears.
You course my soul that I cannot distinguish,
from a basket of ripe berries, brimming,
perfect, every one, impossible to pluck one and
say, *You are the best!*
I savor you all.


## Oppressed Glory

Beleaguered daisy
washed by passing street sweepers,
leans against a tire
abandoned by a cracked road,
green stem with splattered wheel spokes


## Festival Queen

Adorned with silver,
sleigh-borne to the winter fest
where jewelry dazzles beneath
icy azure skies, the queen
waves with courtly grace, all smiles

## A Breath to End It

Crushed by a whisper
uttered as candles flare bright,
tears well and flow free
in mockery of the flames
and their flickering promise


## Tiller

It's time again to hoe the fields;
the water runs and the sun
soars quickly high.  In sweat and toil,
on landscape, hard, he chops and weeds, then
sows and reaps,  his song of life
no idle lullaby to the seasons
as they pass in seeded, hard won yields
of crops that grow to stifle hungry cries—
till peace  in  death,  beyond  his  lasting  sigh,
gives him rest beneath a stone,
fanned by passing butterflies.

## So Rock With Him

When the music man comes,
his songs wafting through
air, citing poems that rhyme
with lyrics that snare,
don't turn him away
with a scoff and a shove,
God may have sent him
with music to love

So rock with him friends
for the gifts that he gives,
the eighth notes, quarter notes,
half notes live.
You sing them with gusto
and love through the night,
slow tempo and quick,
he plays them just right

The distractions are many
as he works with his tunes,
building great love songs
to play you come June,
with all your white veils,
your long traveling trains,
he'll accompany your journey,
God save him, he reigns.

So rock with him friends
for the gifts that he gives,
the eighth notes, quarter notes,
half notes live.
You sing them with gusto
and love through the night,
slow tempo and quick,
he plays them just right

The love is his present,
the songs are his gifts,
he puts them together
with pains and with wit.
Don't think love's secrets
were learned overnight, no,
the perils of research
caused him many a fright.

So rock with him friends
for the gifts that he gives,
the eighth notes, quarter notes,
half notes live.
You sing them with gusto
and love through the night,
slow tempo and quick,
he plays them just right.

## Legacy

"Flash" toddled, giggling, down the ghost
town street, away from her mother's reach;
she won by an arms-length but mom closed the
widening breach.

I watched from the park bench, winded.

Grandma caught up with the struggling pair,
in time lend hands to stop the mad "Flash", who
pointed with passion at a barber pole, dragged
them all laughing, in her mad dash.

I sighed from the park bench, dejected.

Then a deep breath of the earthy town,
gave visions of old families, complete.
My strength returned, pulsing, greater than
before, the  future is assured by care, sweet.

I rose from the park bench, elated.

## *Sentent le vent**

Wind-song or whistle
the composer girds to learn—
wool collar flipped high—
what silvery notes to play—
Life vetted by winter fits

*Fr. Feeling the Wind


## Book of Stars

Peaceful sighs echo
here beneath the canopy signed for the
future—
Evanescent chronicles in brilliant celestial
ink

# Part III

## Synaptic Jump

Comments
strike as they may
to grant pleasure and pain
after leaping across acres
of junctions through Marconi's message code
to both our hearts and fragile souls
the humble, stirring truth
that we must have
comments

## Cosmic Truth

The love
of a husband
for his beautiful wife
is what I express with these lines
for you

Softly
padded passion
without volume limits
within our knowledge of such things
profound

For all
of existence
to resonate tidings
sounded on waves and through portals
unknown

Honest
as purely formed
for the joy of your heart
and diffused as true cosmic truth
our bond

## The Other Side of Here

You've asked me now to accompany you
off to a new frontier
but I'll only venture to the farthest side
of the outermost star, beyond the last galaxy
where we'll stare into purest night then turn
and see the journey we made.
I'll ask you then to accompany me
off to a new frontier, back into purest light.

## From Soul-Depth to Mars

Love of my dreams and my heartache,
how many drops will it cost me?
Swelling banks with hot tears flooding fields
to quell fears?
I'll hold out my hand when I find you.

Oh, let this reach you wherever you are
this love that I send you from soul-depth
to Mars

How will I know when I've found you?
What will you give as your love sign?
Will it be as I've done calling out till I've
won the place in your heart, and you tell
me?

Oh let this reach you wherever you are,
this love that I send you from soul-depth
to Mars

I know we'll grin when we stand there
our cheeks flushed, our words gone,
and our gaze—oh the charm! Laughter soft,
cozy warm. I ask for a dance and we glide
home

Oh let this reach you wherever you are
this love that I send you from soul-depth
to Mars

## Interlude

The adobe stills
as musicians leave to rest;
guttering candles
shadow walls and instruments
left to listen to murmurs

## Strains of Night

Starlit symphony,
crystal clear orchestration
of life after dark—
wood nymphs breathe and flutter leaves
while Jiminy rubs his wings

## Of Sticks and Stones...and Books

Surf with no spray,
dunes with no blowing sand;
hair not mussed by fidgety wind,
regardless the horse's rough gait.
Nor is sweat produced from relentless rays
on vistas, bluish-white—
neither will they make you squint;
a snowstorm wreaks havoc
across a rolling, high-desert plain,
and cattle low for feed not there,
but they're in no danger from hunger or
worse.
Nor are we hurt by slanting, golf ball hail,
the playful child chilled as her bare, blue
hands thrust snowballs skyward to
ruthlessly fly   as one reads with sleepy
eyes, draws air of leather lounge, and
coffee, and sounds of cracking embers
from the fire, nearby; for, we all know,
everything will be righted in the end

## Autumn Fallout

Wavering shadows
accompany quaking leaves
that shed a dandruff
of food for the avid earth—
to encourage next year's green

## Puzzle of the Dark

Of a day yet dawned, black as sin,
with promise only in my mind
for yesterday's rays to return
and light my path again to you,
to meet your eyes, softly shining,
your sweetly scented skin, silky smooth,
I can't wait.
I reach for your shape to be greeted
by a soft, sleeping murmur.
More than ever I yearn for dawn
to savor your heartwarming smile,
and taste your delight in return.

## Sage Reno

Where once grew parched sage
is a city built of gold,
sweat, and tinkling laughs—
it bustles rightfully proud
above sweet scents of the past

## Movement

*Crack!* rends predawn air
widening eyes to strain
and see what moves on black,
grass spears outside...
two deer step with innocent stealth
across the pebbled path,
retreating fleeing shade

## Dogs' Nightly Do

Dogs howl at night as day suspends,
to bark their needs as hearts propend,
they growl at toads, pleased as they may,
sniff green leapers who hop away,
then bark and run and nip with friends.

Atop dewed mounds and past hoar bends
'neath Yang's bright orb through gray mist-
blends,
an owl swoops low, its screeches *fray*—
dogs howl at night

The sun lifts high and clouds ascend,
the fogdog holes clear and amend
dog's need to bark throughout the day,
a break for ears that sorely paid,
dogs land on mats, Man gets his friends—
Dogs howl at night.

## Musician in the Dark

Wistful blues talent
alone in a dusky room
safe with weariness
eases back the recliner
lets New Orleans jazz take her

## Blues Joy

The last note trails on
in a song of endless hope
never quite fulfilled
not sad, but not requited,
pressing her to carry on

## Yearning

Whither wand'rest I
save by the heaving sea
I dream of salt
and roaring surf
and there I long to be

*Curl*, Oil on Canvas, Virginia Ross Circa 1967

**Tree Line Coif**

Sculpture
by erosion
from gales and splintery ice
hallmarks the gnarled bristlecone pine's
presence

**Sunset Farewell**

Shadows
trail sloping ground
ever longer, deepening
as night falls, day loathe to vacate
its claim

**One Dog's Toy**

A wallet
rests with my dog
beneath a marble stone
because he liked to play with it
and me

**So Final**

Petals slip and slide
on transparent air currents
loathe to land in Fall

## My Love Greets Another You

*Then* and *now*--
two words back to back,
duel on an artificial line
painted on a Mobius strip
that clocks us as we pass and pass again.
The paper path decries
we'll always be the same, as
it plays its twisted game in

places cuddled to themselves with
grandparents there,
and parents here, while Bobby and Habib,
in a bubble of laughter, play on the hill
behind places where they sleep, unaware
the growls of bulldozer sweeps
that scrape to make tomorrow.

Sometimes I almost see the seam that
doesn't exist in seamless time--when
carpenters hammer additions to the house
that was said to be large enough for any
family, ten years ago . . . when
the seam winks at me and lets food that
never tasted good before, startle my
palette with delight.

I reach into a scented drawer and slide a
picture out, to stare. It's Grandma who
cradles, with infinite care, our precious
newborn girl. Suddenly,
baby powder scents fantasy air-- and I
almost sneeze.
Grandma, bless her soul and boundless
love, is gone.

Her memory smiles from the glossy print—
one seam of *then* and *now* that tugs my
heart, quite clear.

I greet you in your yellow dress, so
stunning a change from your usual one of
azure hue.
I kiss your soft, sweet lips to seal my love,
again;
then snap a photo while
your joyful eyes dance on this windy day—
now captured in wildflower hue. I hope to
slide it from another scented drawer one
day very soon, and feel my blood run warm
that day, when *then* is *now*, your image,
*now* as *then*.

## Space

That which touches all but doesn't care
supports us all but has no air
no eye to see no hands to feel no need to
eat but is so real
it holds the planets, spins the stars,
gives us glimpses, oh, so far, of more and
more and more

We'll travel through it, all that way,
someday, to wherever we want on ships
without sail, on waves of sinuous nothing
supporting our journey, ether that's
everywhere in that glorious void,
that substance of nothing that's really
something

## Romantic Trappings

Diamonds
and women gleam
when ensembled for night
and reflected by candlelight
across a table contracted by eyes
that sparkle behind golden flames
with a murmur of love
that passes through
diamonds

# Index of First Lines

A native of California, a graduate of Missouri State University, and a globe-trotting student of mankind, Jim has taken myriad inspirations and applied them to novels (*Sport of Hearts, Kid Me You Die*), won a Writer's International Network Award for his short story, *Sparkling Water, Twinkling Eyes*, and is currently developing a television pilot.

www.ingramcontent.com/pod-product-compliance
Lightning Source LLC
Chambersburg PA
CBHW041025170626
46815CB00001B/5